POISONOUS
PLANTS

Poisonous Plants

by PETER R. LIMBURG

Illustrated by Marjorie Zaum

Julian Messner New York

Library of Congress Cataloging in Publication Data

Limburg, Peter R.
    Poisonous plants.

    1. Poisonous plants. I. Zaum, Marjorie. II. Title.
QK100.A1L55   582'.06'9   76-25804
ISBN 0-671-32805-0 lib. bdg.

Contents

Plants of Woods, Fields, and Roadsides

Introduction

When I started doing research for this book, I was surprised to learn how many plants are poisonous—or can be, under the wrong conditions. Some plants, such as poison ivy and deadly nightshade, are outright poisonous. But many seemingly harmless plants, such as the oak, can be poisonous to animals that eat too much of the young leaves and buds. Probably oak leaves would poison humans, too, if we ate them.

Even parts of some of the plants we eat every day are poisonous. For example, the leaves of rhubarb, the leaves and stems of tomato plants, and the seeds of apples are poisonous. There is a famous case of a man who loved apple seeds so much that he decided to save them until he had enough for a real treat. When he had saved a whole cupful, he sat down to enjoy them. Before the cup was finished, the man was dead. The cause of death was cyanide, a poisonous natural chemical found in the seeds of apples, pears, peaches, and plums.

How poisonous are the plants we discuss in this book? The question is a tricky one. The toxicity (poisonousness) of a plant often varies according to the season of the year, the kind of soil it is growing in, and the amount of rain and sunshine it has gotten. And people vary in their reactions to plant poisons, too. Some can stand a larger dose than others.

Most of the plants described are not deadly. Some of them cause skin rashes. Others cause severe intestinal or stomach upsets—vomiting and diarrhea. But some cause death, if a large amount is swallowed. And in some cases, only a small amount is enough to kill.

Some of these plants you will most likely find in woods and fields, or along roadsides. Some are grown in the United States mainly as indoor plants. Most of them are garden plants, although you may find them growing wild or in pots inside the house.

What should you do if someone suddenly becomes ill, and you think he or she has been poisoned by a plant? Try to find out what plants or fruits the victim has eaten in the last few hours. Do your best to get the plants, or at least a few of the leaves. Try to make the person vomit, if he or she is not doing so already. But do not try to treat the victim yourself. Get him or her to the doctor as quickly as possible. And bring along your sample of the plant or plants you think caused the poisoning. This is important because it will help the doctor identify the plant and choose the correct treatment. If the victim ate more than one kind of plant, try to bring samples of all of them. The sooner the victim is treated, the better. So being able to identify the plant promptly may save somebody's life.

We don't give a list of treatments here for two reasons. For one thing, treating a case of plant poisoning often requires medicines that people don't have in their homes. For another, people without medical training might make mistakes, and leave the victim worse off than before. So leave treatment to the doctor. After all, that's what a doctor is trained for.

Many poisonous plants add beauty to our gardens and parks. Others give us valuable products such as medicinal drugs. This book was not written to frighten you, or to make you shy away from these plants, nor to make you rip them out of the garden. It was written to give you the knowledge you need to enjoy these interesting plants safely.

House Plants

AMARYLLIS

AMARYLLIS, also called belladonna lily, is a lily-like plant that is native to South Africa. In the warmest parts of the United States, it can be grown as an outdoor flower, but in most parts of the country it is a house plant.

Although it looks like a big lily, amaryllis does not belong to the lily family. It belongs to its own family—the amaryllis family—along with such plants as the daffodil (also called narcissus), the cactus-like agave, or century plant, and a prickly weed called *lechuguilla,* which grows in the Southwest. *Lechuguilla* is Spanish for "little lettuce," but it is not good to put in a salad. Not only are its leaves spiny; it is poisonous.

An amaryllis plant has leaves shaped like a long, pointed tongue. The leaves may grow to a foot and a half in length. The flowers grow on a long stem that comes up between the leaves. Most amaryllises are red or pink, but there are also varieties of other colors.

The dangerous part of an amaryllis is the bulb, which looks like an oversized onion. The bulb contains chemicals that cause severe digestive upsets. Even a few bites can make trouble.

Amaryllis was a name that ancient Greek and Latin poets used for pretty girls in their poems. About 200 years ago, the great Swedish botanist Carolus Linnaeus, who invented the modern system of classifying plants, gave this name to the new, popular flower from South Africa.

CALADIUM

CALADIUM is a plant with large, showy leaves colored green-and-white, green-and-pink, green-and-red, all red, and other combinations of these colors. Caladiums are native to the tropics of South America, but in the United States and Canada they are grown as house plants. In summer, caladiums are also grown in outdoor gardens, and in the warmer parts of the United States, they can be grown outdoors all year round.

Caladiums are not the sort of plant people would normally think of as food. But little children, who will put almost anything in their mouths, may nibble on the leaves. When cats are lonely and bored, they, too, often nibble on house plants.

But children and pets soon learn a painful lesson. Caladiums contain needle-sharp crystals of calcium oxalate, a chemical. Anyone who chews on them gets a mouthful of these slivers. It is like biting into a pincushion with invisible pins. Swallowing the plant buries more of the crystals in the lining of the throat and stomach. Mouth and throat are left raw and burning. The intestines may also be hurt.

Caladium belongs to the arum family, which is important to know about because so many ornamental house plants belong to that family. All of them contain the dangerous crystals of calcium oxalate. Perhaps the plants evolved this way as a protection against being eaten.

CROTON

CROTON, a native of southeast Asia, is grown for its beautiful foliage of many-colored leaves of red, green, and yellow. In regions where it is warm all year round, the croton grows up to six feet high.

The croton belongs to the spurge family, and its leaves contain a poison that causes diarrhea and vomiting if swallowed. It may also blister the mouth and tongue.

Croton has several relatives that grow wild in the United States. The American varieties of croton are not ornamental like their Asian cousin. In fact, they look quite weedy. The American crotons like dry, sandy soil; so you won't run into them at a lake shore or in a swamp.

One of the American wild crotons is the woolly croton, which is also called "hogwort." It grows from 1½ to 4 feet tall, and its stems are covered with woolly hairs, which is what gives it its name. The Texas croton is about half the size of the woolly croton. Both kinds are poisonous. Animals grazing in the fields tend to leave them alone because the plants have a dreadful smell and taste. But cattle have been poisoned by eating them when they are in hay.

The name *croton* is Greek for "tick," not the sound made by a clock, but the tiny bloodsucking insect that bothers dogs, cattle, horses, humans and other warm-blooded creatures. The name was given to the plant because some scientist thought that its seeds resembled ticks gorged with blood. (A tick swells up to the size of a baked bean when

it is full.) And it is these seeds that are the most dangerous part of the croton plant. They contain a very powerful, oily poison, so strong that it destroys the skin tissue
and causes scars.

Croton oil was once used in medicine as a purgative (a
drug that "cleans out" the patient by causing vomiting and
violent bowel movements). Because of its strength, croton
oil had to be mixed with other liquids to dilute it, and it
was given in very small quantities. Doctors no longer use
croton oil. They have better and safer drugs.

DUMB CANE

DUMB CANE got its name
not because it is a stupid
plant, but because it is likely
to strike dumb (speechless)
anyone who bites into it.
The reason for this is that
the plant is full of needle-
sharp crystals of calcium oxalate, a chemical.

Biting into the plant
is something like biting into
a porcupine. The needles
bury themselves in the tongue and mouth, causing intense pain and burning. The
pain becomes even worse
when the victim tries to
move his tongue and lips to form words. Every year, fool-
ish people chew dumb cane, either on a dare or to see what
will happen. They get a painful lesson.

In almost all cases, the irritation goes away after a few
days and does no permanent harm. But sometimes the victim's tongue swells up so badly that it blocks the breathing

passages, and he or she chokes to death.

Dumb cane's scientific name is *Dieffenbachia* (for the German scientist, Ernst Dieffenbach, who described it). It belongs to the arum family, like caladium, skunk cabbage, and jack-in-the-pulpit. Dumb cane is native to the tropics, but it is a popular house plant in the United States because it doesn't need sunlight to grow.

Dumb cane has a long, slender stem with light brown bark. The stem bends so easily that it has to be fastened to a stake or the plant will fall over. The long, glossy green leaves, splotched with white or yellow, sprout from the top of the stem. It is an attractive plant, and perfectly harmless as long as you don't try to chew it.

JERUSALEM CHERRY

JERUSALEM CHERRY is a member of the nightshade family. It is a popular house plant around Christmas time because its cherry-like fruits ripen and turn a bright shade of red.

All parts of the plant are poisonous, and they contain three poisons. The poisons may cause vomiting and diarrhea, or they may attack the nervous system, paralyzing the muscles and causing unconsciousness. People have died from eating Jerusalem cherries.

The nightshade family is a large one, containing some of our most important food plants, such as tomato, potato, and green pepper. But many plants in this family are poisonous.

LANTANA

LANTANA is a member of the verbena or vervain family, and comes from the tropical parts of North, Central, and South America. It is prized for its colorful flowers of yellow, orange, lavender, and rose. In the North, lantana is grown as a house plant for a touch of color in winter. In the warmer parts of the South and in California, it is grown as an outdoor plant. In places, lantana grows into a shrub from 3 to 5 feet tall.

In Hawaii, lantana, brought in as a garden plant, went wild. It is now a serious pest, forming jungle-like thickets and crowding out native plants. It also grows wild in the warmest parts of the mainland United States.

Unfortunately, this plant with the lovely flowers contains some very dangerous chemicals. Farm animals that eat lantana become photosensitized. This means that their skins cannot stand light. A photosensitized animal's skin becomes red and inflamed and puffy when exposed to light. It is extremely painful. Lantana poisoning can also cause horrible sores on the skins of animals, and may also destroy their livers.

In human beings, lantana causes severe diarrhea and intestinal irritation. It also makes the body's muscles very weak until the effects of the poison wear off. The lantana plant bears berry-like fruits the size of a pea which are greenish-blue or black in color. Children have died from eating these poisonous fruits.

16

MISTLETOE

MISTLETOE. Around Christmas time, many people hang a sprig of a deadly plant in their homes—mistletoe!

Mistletoe is an unusual plant. It grows as a parasite on oaks and other trees, stealing nourishment from them and giving nothing in return. In some parts of Europe and North America, mistletoe is a serious pest, which weakens trees and deforms them.

In ancient times, people considered the mistletoe magical, partly because it grows in the branches of a tree instead of in the ground, and partly because its leaves stay green all winter. People used to carry pieces of mistletoe in their pockets as charms against evil. They would also fasten mistletoe branches over the doors of houses and barns to keep out witches and demons.

Mistletoe's magic power was supposed to be strongest if the plant was gathered at midsummer or Christmas. This is probably why today we have the tradition of using mistletoe in Christmas decorations.

The poisonous part of mistletoe is its sticky, whitish berries, which cause severe intestinal upsets. In a big enough dose, they can cause death from exhaustion after hours of very painful suffering. After going through hours of vomiting and diarrhea, some people are so worn out that their bodies do not have enough strength to go on living. People have also died from drinking a tea made from mistletoe berries. They may have been trying out one of the old folk medicine recipes. There is a risk that small children and pets may eat the berries, particularly if they come loose and drop on the floor.

Several native species of mistletoe grow wild in various parts of the United States. Practically all the mistletoe we see in Christmas decorations is a kind called American mistletoe, which is the state flower of Oklahoma.

Mistletoe is poisonous to cats, cattle, and many other animals, besides human beings. But birds love the berries and feast on them unharmed. In fact, birds are the chief spreaders of mistletoe seeds.

PHILODENDRON

PHILODENDRON is a vine with smooth, heart-shaped leaves that is grown as a house plant in the United States. It is very popular because it is easy to grow and, as a native of tropical rain forests, can stand a great deal of shade. It also grows fast, and people like to see quick results with their plants.

The name *philodendron* is Greek for "tree-lover." In their native rain forests, some kinds of philodendrons do love to climb up trees. But the kinds grown in the United States have soft-stemmed, trailing vines that need to be fastened to supports to keep them off the floor.

Philodendron belongs to the poisonous arum family. It is not as dangerous as dumb cane, but eating it is not recommended. Philodendron is one of the main causes of poisoning in cats, and should be kept out of their reach.

POINSETTIA

POINSETTIA is raised for its bright-red "flowers." Actually these are *bracts*—a special kind of leaf. The real flowers are tiny, yellow blossoms that grow in the center of the circle of red bracts. (Some varieties of poinsettia have white bracts.)

Poinsettia belongs to the spurge family, and its milky juice contains irritating substances that cause digestive upsets or blistering of the mouth if parts of the plant are chewed or swallowed. The juice may also irritate the skin. Small children sometimes think the red "petals" look good enough to eat. So be sure your younger brothers and sisters don't eat them. Pets, too, sometimes nibble on poinsettia.

Poinsettia comes originally from Mexico and Central America where it grows as a wild shrub. It blossoms in the winter, which is the rainy season in its native area. Summers are hot and dry, and the plant drops its leaves and "hibernates" until the rains come again.

The plant is named for an American statesman, Joel Roberts Poinsett. Poinsett was born in Charleston, S.C., in 1779, and went into politics as an adult.

In 1826, he was named ambassador to Mexico. In between his official duties, he sometimes went out into the countryside to study the plants, for he was interested in science. Unfortunately, Poinsett did something no diplomat should ever do. He got involved in the politics of the country he was sent to. The politicians whom Poinsett was helping lost, and the winners forced him to leave the country.

In 1828 he took back to Charleston with him a plant called "flame leaf," or lobster flower. There he bred varieties with bigger flowers, like the ones we have today. At first, the variety Poinsett bred was called American Easter flower. But in 1836, the plant was renamed poinsettia, in honor of Poinsett.

One of poinsettia's relatives, the crown-of-thorns, is also a popular house plant, and it contains the same poison. Fortunately, its bristly stems discourage small children from trying to find out how it tastes.

Plants of Gardens and Yards

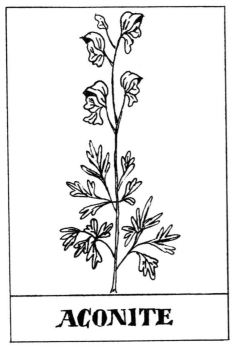

ACONITE

ACONITE is a member of the buttercup family. (*See* Buttercup.) Unlike most kinds of buttercup plants, which have yellow flowers, aconites have deep-blue flowers. The plants are grown in gardens, and grow 3 to 4 feet tall.

Aconite contains two powerful nerve poisons. These poisons affect the muscles so that they become weak and powerless and interfere with breathing. The poisons also make the heart beat slowly and irregularly. People have died after eating aconite. Although all parts of the plant are poisonous, the most deadly parts are the roots and seeds.

Aconite has been known as a poisonous plant since ancient times. An old name for it in Europe was "wolfsbane," for people thought it killed wolves. In fact, some people even believed that just smelling the flowers was deadly. (It really isn't.) Another name, still used today, is "monkshood." This name comes from the hood-shaped top petal of the flowers.

Some kinds of aconite grow wild in the United States. They grow up to 6 feet tall, with yellow flowers. Like most of the other plants of the buttercup family, they like moist or marshy soil. They are just as poisonous as the garden aconites.

Closely related to aconite is larkspur, a popular garden plant with flowers of blue, purple, pink, or white. The larkspur grown in American gardens is descended from a kind found in Europe. But there are more than a dozen kinds of native American larkspur that grow wild, especially in the West. Experts say that they are among the most dangerous plants on the range. More cattle are killed by eating larkspur than by any other plant except locoweed.

AUTUMN CROCUS

AUTUMN CROCUS, or meadow saffron, a native of Europe, is raised as a garden plant in the United States. Despite its name, it is not a true crocus. In fact, it does not even belong to the same family as the crocuses. True crocuses are members of the iris family; autumn crocus is in the lily family. Many gardeners know it better under its scientific name of *Colchicum*.

In early autumn, the leaves of the autumn crocus sprout from the plant's underground bulb. In a few weeks, the leaves wither and die. Only then do the flowers, white or light purple in color, appear.

The bulb, leaves, and flowers contain two poisons. One is *veratrine*, which is also found in false hellebore. (*See* False Hellebore.) The other is *colchicine*, which has very powerful effects on the body. A pinch of powdered colchicine on the skin causes pain. If swallowed, it causes intense pain, vomiting, diarrhea, bleeding inside the body, and sometimes death.

Yet in very small doses, colchicine is a valuable drug. For hundreds of years, it has been used to treat the disease known as gout, a crippling, painful ailment in the joints of the toes and fingers. Colchicine has also contributed a great deal to scientific research with animal and plant cells. Some of our improved plants of farm and garden have been created with the aid of colchicine.

But people have been killed by too large a dose of the drug. And in Europe, where the plant grows wild, farm animals have been killed by eating hay with autumn crocus leaves in it.

BOXWOOD

BOXWOOD and PRIVET are two very common hedge plants. They are not related, but both are highly poisonous.

Boxwood is an evergreen shrub with small, roundish, shiny leaves. Although it is native to Europe and Asia, it is grown in the milder parts of the United States (cold winters kill it). Boxwood can be clipped into all kinds of fanciful shapes such as animals, birds, geometric figures.

Boxwood has a disagreeable smell and a bitter taste that discourages people from eating it. Farm animals have been poisoned by it, however. The plant contains alkaloids that cause severe vomiting and diarrhea, and may kill the victim quickly by causing suffocation.

Privet, a native of Europe and Asia, is planted practically all over the United States and much of Canada, as it stands cold much better than boxwood. Depending on the species, privet grows from 3 to 30 feet tall if left untrimmed. Privet belongs to the olive family, and its relatives include the ash tree, from which baseball bats are made, and the forsythia bush, whose yellow flowers are one of the earliest signs of spring.

Privet poisoning is rare, but children in Europe have been poisoned by it. Botanists have not yet identified the poison, but they know it causes severe irritation of stomach and intestines, pain, vomiting, and diarrhea. Victims may die of exhaustion. Horses, cattle, and sheep have died from eating privet leaves and clippings from hedges.

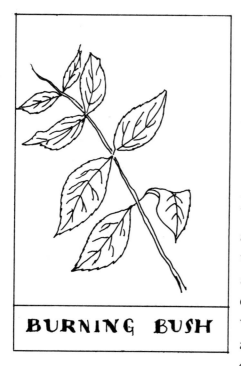

BURNING BUSH

BURNING BUSH is a name given to several different plants whose leaves turn bright colors in the fall. There are two you should know about.

One is the winged burning bush, which came originally from China. It grows to be 8 or 9 feet tall and nearly as wide. In fall, its leaves turn a very bright red, and it also has scarlet berries. It is easy to recognize because winglike ridges of bark grow along its twigs. It is a popular ornamental plant for yards, and in parts of the country it grows wild where birds have carried the seeds.

The other burning bush is a native American cousin, which is also called by the Indian name of wahoo (meaning "arrow wood"). The wahoo grows in eastern North America and can reach the height of a medium-sized tree, 25 feet tall. In fall, the wahoo's leaves turn bright yellow. Its fruits are scarlet.

Both bushes contain a substance that acts like a very harsh laxative. It may also cause vomiting and drowsiness. Children have been poisoned by eating the berries and leaves. Farm animals have been poisoned by browsing on the bark and roots. However, birds can eat the fruits without harm.

Some American Indian tribes used to make a laxative drink by boiling the bark from the roots of the wahoo. White settlers copied them, and for a long time wahoo was a favorite home remedy. But one of the troubles with home remedies is that it is hard to be sure of their strength, and it is easy to give a dangerous overdose.

Another plant called "burning bush" is *Kochia scoparia,* which is the botanists' way of saying "Koch's broomlike plant." Kochia is also called "fireball" and "summer cypress." In autumn, its leaves turn bright red. It is much used in gardens as a screen to hide ugly objects. Kochia can photosensitize animals that eat it—that is, make them oversensitive to sunlight, which poisons them. But it is not known to have poisoned any humans.

CASTOR-OIL PLANT

CASTOR-OIL PLANT, or castor-bean plant. Millions of people around the world have taken castor oil as a laxative. Horrible as its taste is, castor oil is no more dangerous than any other strong laxative. But the plant itself is poisonous, and the seeds—often called "castor beans"—are extremely poisonous.

The castor-oil plant belongs to the spurge family. It is a native of tropical parts of Africa, where it grows into a full-sized tree nearly 40 feet tall. But in the United States and Canada, it grows only 6 to 8 feet tall. It is usually raised as an ornamental plant in gardens. (An ornamental plant is one that people raise just for its looks.) With their huge, lush, spreading leaves, castor-oil plants make a good, quick-growing screen.

The leaves are green, but often they are tinted pink or red. The flowers are small. The seeds grow in soft, burr-like pods. When ripe, the seeds look like shiny beans, about two-fifths of an inch long and black or mottled gray and brown in color.

The seeds are very oily, and castor oil is made by pressing them. In the United States, the seeds are roasted before pressing the oil out. This destroys the poison that the oil carries. But in many countries, the seeds are pressed without roasting, and the oil in this case is poisonous.

The poison is a very complicated protein called *ricin*

(from *Ricinus,* the scientific name of the castor-oil plant). Ricin is a blood poison and also upsets the body chemistry. The body absorbs the poison through the walls of the intestines and even through the skin.

Victims of castor-oil poisoning first feel a burning sensation in their mouths and throats. Then come vomiting, diarrhea, and thirst. Vision is blurred. The victims become weak, and then collapse. Sometimes their hearts beat violently. So powerful is the poison that a single seed, if chewed and swallowed, will make a small child ill and may even cause death. Eight seeds will kill most adults.

More than 2,000 years ago, people around the Mediterranean Sea were raising the castor-oil plant. The ancient Egyptians and Hebrews had a name for the plant that meant "nauseous-tasting." They used the oil for several purposes. They burned it in lamps to light their houses; they used it for rubdowns and skin ointments; and they used it as a laxative. They must have known enough to roast the seeds before pressing the oil to make it safe.

Today castor-oil plants are raised commercially in the warmer parts of the world. A small crop of it is even grown in the southern United States and California. But only a small part of the crop is used to make laxatives. The main use for the oil is in industry, for it is an excellent lubricant. (A lubricant is a substance like oil or grease. It lets moving parts slide smoothly and easily over each other.) Castor oil has a special advantage. It does not attack rubber and cause it to rot, as ordinary oil does.

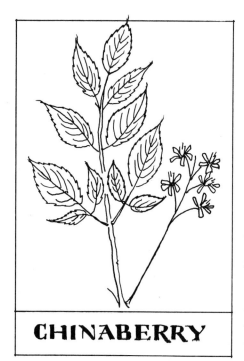

CHINABERRY

CHINABERRY. A familiar sight in the southern United States is the chinaberry tree, with its smooth, shiny, yellow fruits. These fruits gave the tree its name because they look as if they were made of china. Native to Syria, Iran, and India, the chinaberry tree was brought to the United States as an ornamental plant in the first half of the 1800s. It cannot live in the cold winters of the North and West, but it does well in the climate of the South. It does so well there that it has gone wild.

The chinaberry tree, which belongs to the mahogany family, grows 30 to 45 feet tall. Its spreading branches provide cool, deep shade for the hot Southern summers. In season, it bears large quantities of purple flowers, which are followed by half-inch berrylike fruits. The flowers have a strong, sweet scent—some people find it almost too strong.

The flowers, leaves, and bark of the chinaberry, and especially the berries, contain a poison that acts in two ways. It can produce severe intestinal upsets, or it can cause difficulty in breathing, paralysis, and death. Even when they do not die, victims recover slowly.

In the United States, some people—mostly children —have died from chinaberry poisoning. Scientists believe that not all varieties of the tree are poisonous; so perhaps a nonpoisonous kind will someday be available. Meanwhile, you had better treat all chinaberries as dangerous.

CHRISTMAS ROSE

CHRISTMAS ROSE is not a rose at all, but a relative of the buttercup. Its scientific name is *Helleborus*. This is the name the ancient Greeks gave the plant. It is raised as an ornamental garden plant. As its name suggests, it blooms around Christmas time. Its white or dark-reddish flowers are the only ones you will see blooming outdoors at that time of year—unless you live in a place with a very mild climate. Another variety of Christmas rose blooms in early spring instead of midwinter.

The Christmas rose contains a poison that causes digestive upsets. It may also attack the nervous system. In severe cases, it causes ringing in the ears, dizziness, thirst, and a feeling of suffocation. It has been known to cause death by stopping the heart.

The thick, fleshy roots are the most dangerous part of the plant. The roots are covered with a blackish-brown skin. For this reason, many people call the plant *black hellebore*. (There is also a white hellebore and a false hellebore, which is native to North America.)

For at least two thousand years, people have known that the Christmas rose is poisonous. In fact, the ancient Greeks had a nickname for the roots: "bread of death." Yet the Greeks sometimes dried the roots, crushed them to powder, and sniffed them up their noses. The purpose was to quicken their wits.

An extract of Christmas-rose roots was once used by

doctors to treat the mentally ill—that was in the days when these people were thought to be possessed by demons. The idea was that if you treated the poor mentally ill patient brutally enough, the demon would get tired of taking so much punishment and would go away. One result of the old-fashioned treatment was that few mentally ill persons recovered their sanity. Another was that many of them died of the treatment.

Christmas rose was also once used to treat children for worms. But as one old-time writer pointed out, it usually killed the child as well as the worms. Fortunately, it is no longer used in medicine.

DAFFODIL

DAFFODIL. One of the most popular spring flowers is the daffodil, or trumpet narcissus. (*Narcissus* is its scientific name.) A native of southern Europe, the daffodil is a garden flower in the United States and Canada. If you should see a stand of daffodils apparently growing wild in the woods, the chances are that they are a last reminder that a house once stood there. Daffodils growing near a roadside are probably there because someone tossed some worn-out bulbs away.

However, daffodil bulbs are dangerous because they contain substances that cause vomiting, diarrhea, and sometimes trembling or convulsions. Children have been poisoned by eating daffodil bulbs that their parents left around the house before planting them.

Interestingly, field mice and other small wild animals very seldom eat daffodil bulbs, though they eat plenty of other flowering bulbs. Perhaps they recognize that daffodil bulbs are poisonous.

The name *daffodil* comes from "asphodel," the name of a flower that grows wild around the Mediterranean Sea. *Narcissus* was the name of a character in Greek mythology. Narcissus was an extremely handsome young man, so handsome that men and women alike fell hopelessly in love with him. But Narcissus was cold-hearted and conceited, and cared only for himself. He was cruel to everyone who loved him. Finally, the gods punished him by leading him to a forest pool, where he fell in love with his own reflection. Trying to reach the handsome youth he saw in the pool, Narcissus fell in and was drowned. In another version of the legend, Narcissus stabbed himself in despair, and the flowers named after him sprang up where his blood had fallen on the ground.

However, some experts think that *narcissus* comes from the same Greek root-word as *narcotic*—that is, *narke,* meaning "numb." In fact, the ancient Greeks made a pain-killing preparation from narcissus. This is believable when we realize that narcissus (daffodil) belongs to the amaryllis family, and that many plants of this family do contain poisons that act like narcotics.

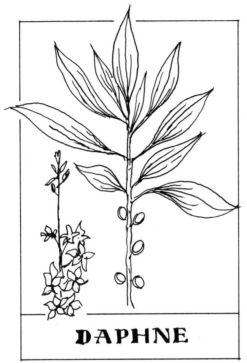

DAPHNE

DAPHNE is a shrub that is raised for its sweet-smelling, fragrant flowers. There are several species of daphne, but two kinds are generally grown in gardens. One is *Daphne mezereum*, which is a bush that grows up to 4 feet tall, with rosy-purple flowers. The other is *Daphne cneorum*, a low, cushiony shrub only 8 to 12 inches tall, with pink blossoms. Gardeners have also developed varieties with white and blue flowers.

Daphne is native to parts of Europe and Asia. It belongs to the mezereum family, which includes the native American plant called wicopy, or leatherwood. The daphnes have taken well to life in America, so much so that some have escaped from cultivation and grow wild in parts of the northeastern United States.

The whole plant is poisonous, but the most dangerous part is its bright-red, shiny berries, which are very attractive to small children. The berries are so bitter that most people would spit them right out. But small children may not know enough to do this, and instead they may swallow the bad-tasting berries.

If they swallow the berries, their stomachs and intestines will be affected. The results are vomiting, diarrhea, bleeding, and sometimes convulsions and death. Even if they spit the berries out immediately, they will still have painfully inflamed lips, mouth, and throat.

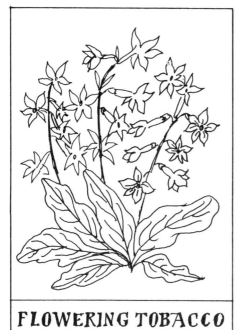

FLOWERING TOBACCO

FLOWERING TOBACCO is an ornamental cousin of the kind of tobacco that is smoked in pipes, cigars, and cigarettes. Like its well-known relative, it is very poisonous, for it contains the narcotic called nicotine.

The name *nicotine* and the tobacco plant's scientific name of *Nicotiana* come from the same source: a French diplomat named Jean Nicot. Nicot lived some 400 years ago, and he has gone down in history as the man who introduced tobacco to France. When Nicot was serving as the French consul in Portugal, a friend gave him a present of tobacco.

By this time, Europeans had heard of tobacco, and some had even seen it. Columbus brought tobacco back from the West Indies after his first voyage in 1492. He told how the Indians "drank the smoke" of dried tobacco leaves. But Europeans had not yet taken up smoking themselves.

Nicot gave some of his tobacco to the king and queen of Portugal, hoping to gain their favor. The royal couple were delighted.

The following year Nicot gave some tobacco to the queen of France. There is a story—no one knows whether it is really true—that the queen of France had a dreadful headache that her doctors could not cure. Nicot gave her a pinch of snuff (tobacco ground to a fine powder) and advised her to sniff it. The queen did so, sneezed violently

—and her headache was cured! True story or not, snuff-taking and then smoking were soon all the rage in France.

People in Europe began to plant tobacco. Although it wasn't as good as the American tobacco, at least they didn't have to pay for shipping it across thousands of miles of ocean. Since tobacco plants have attractive, sweet-scented flowers, people often grew them for ornament. In time, they found that some kinds of tobacco were better for flowers than for smoking. Today's flowering tobaccos are descended from these plants, plus other species that were discovered later.

Besides smoking tobacco, the Indians used it as medicine. They chewed the leaves to dull the pain of a toothache and to make a poultice for sores. They drank tobacco-leaf tea for stomach cramps, and some of them inhaled the smoke to cure their asthma. A strange cure indeed, since people with asthma have trouble breathing, and tobacco smoke makes people choke and cough!

Europeans quickly invented many new "medicinal" uses for tobacco. Few worked, but tobacco was still as good as most other old-time drugs, which did not work either.

If tobacco did any good at all, it was probably chewed to deaden mouth or teeth pain, due to the narcotic action of its nicotine. But if swallowed, tobacco produces vomiting, diarrhea, and worse effects. The nicotine acts on the nervous system, causing the victim to tremble, stagger, and finally collapse.

Many a young person, trying to show off by chewing or smoking tobacco, has suffered some of these symptoms, becoming violently sick to his or her stomach. A few people have died from swallowing too large an amount. Animals are seldom poisoned by eating tobacco. They rarely touch it because of its unpleasant taste.

FOXGLOVE

FOXGLOVE. An old legend tells how God created foxglove to protect foxes from hunters. When the hunters were on the trail, the long, bell-shaped blossoms of the foxglove would ring, warning the foxes.

Actually, foxes have nothing to do with foxglove at all. But the plant, which is native to Europe, has been used in poisons and medicines for hundreds of years. Witches used foxglove as an ingredient in magical potions. Herb doctors boiled the flowers in butter to make a salve for a skin disease called *scrofula* (swelling of glands).

Nearly 200 years ago, an English doctor found that a tea of foxglove leaves helped patients with *dropsy*. Dropsy is the piling up of fluid usually in the patient's legs and lower body. The swelling makes it hard for the patient to move. One of the causes of dropsy is a weak heart. The weak heart cannot keep the blood flowing normally in order to get rid of the fluid. So it piles up where gravity pulls it. But if the patient is given foxglove, a substance in the leaves acts on the heart to pump the blood more strongly so it can carry the large amounts of fluid to the kidneys. Foxglove also helps the kidneys get rid of the excess water in the patient's body.

When scientists finally learned what the wonder-working substance in foxglove was, they named it *digitalis*. This is also the scientific name of the foxglove. It comes from the medieval Latin word for "thimble," and refers to the shape of the flowers.

Unfortunately, the drug digitalis is poisonous in too large a dose. Results range from nausea and diarrhea to pounding of the heart, drowsiness, and even convulsions.

Foxglove was brought to the United States and Canada by early settlers from Europe. It is raised as a garden flower in almost every part of the United States, and in some places it has gone wild. Wild foxglove has purple or white flowers. Garden varieties come in many colors.

Human beings are seldom poisoned by eating foxglove, but a number of people have been poisoned by taking an overdose of medicine made from it. Farm animals have been killed by grazing on foxglove plants in a field or eating them in hay.

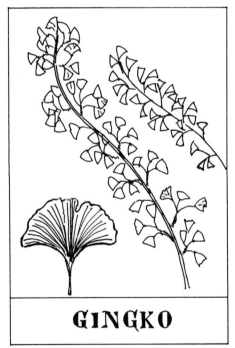

GINGKO

GINKGO is a tree that once grew over large parts of the northern hemisphere. It dates back to the time of the dinosaurs, but something wiped out most of them hundreds of thousands of years ago. Ginkgo trees survived only in China. Monks planted them around temples, and worked hard at keeping the species alive.

The first ginkgo trees were brought to the United States in 1784 to be planted along city streets. They turned out to be immune to plant diseases and unappetizing to insects. They also turned out to be among the few trees that can withstand city fumes and smog. Today they are one of the chief shade trees in the nation.

Ginkgos have separate male and female trees. The females have yellow, olive-sized fruits which contain poison that causes severe skin rashes in many people. However, the seeds of the fruit are edible, and in China they are eaten like nuts.

HOLLY

HOLLY. To many families, Christmas would not be Christmas without a wreath of dark, shiny green holly leaves with their bright red berries. But the berries contain a bitter substance that causes violent vomiting and diarrhea. Small children and cats are especially likely to eat the berries, so the holly should be kept safely out of their reach.

The holly family has members in Europe, Asia, and North America. Most hollies are shrubs or small trees, but in the southern United States one species can grow 100 feet tall if left alone. Some people plant hollies in their yards. Hollies grow wild as far north as southern New Jersey, but they cannot stand severe winters, and they need protection to survive further north. Some species have black berries instead of red.

The wood of the holly plant is hard, heavy, and ivory-white. It can be dyed any sort of color, so it is used a great deal in furniture and inlays. It is also used for black piano keys. Because it is very even-grained, woodcarvers like it.

Some Indian tribes used holly in medicine. One species, called yaupon, that grows in the southeast was used to make a drink that was an extremely powerful purgative. The Creek Indians drank it to purify themselves before important religious ceremonies.

LILY OF THE VALLEY

LILY OF THE VALLEY is a popular garden plant because of its sweet-scented, white, bell-shaped flowers. If insects pollinate the flowers, they produce red berries about one-half inch in diameter.

All parts of the plant contain a poison that acts on the heart like digitalis, the active ingredient of foxglove. They have seldom caused deaths because the leaves are so bitter that farm animals do not eat them.

The berries, too, are bitter. Most curious humans who try one spit it out before any harm is done. But occasionally someone does swallow one or more berries, and dies.

There is also a report of a small girl who drank the water from a vase in which a bouquet of lily of the valley flowers was standing. The sap of the cut stems, seeping into the water, was enough to kill her.

LOBELIA

LOBELIA is named for a man who probably never saw one, a French-born botanist named Matthias de Lobel. Lobel died in 1616, and the first lobelia specimens from North America probably did not reach Europe until after that date. But he was such a famous botanist that the new plant was named in his honor.

Lobelias grow in Africa, Asia, and South America as well as North America. The giant of the family, a towering 30-footer, grows in the remote Ruwenzori Mountains, in east central Africa. The smallest member of the family, a 12-inch plant, comes from the Cape of Good Hope, at Africa's southern tip.

There are three chief species of American lobelias. One has a brilliant-red flower and grows to 5 feet tall. Equally tall is the blue lobelia. The third species is the 3-foot *Lobelia inflata,* which is often called Indian tobacco because the Indians smoked its leaves as a substitute for tobacco. The first two grow in moist places; Indian tobacco prefers open woods and fields. But you are more likely to encounter lobelias in a garden, for they are very popular garden flowers.

Each of these lobelias causes vomiting and diarrhea. A big dose also causes sweating, pain, paralysis, lowered body temperature, and collapse.

The Indians used all three lobelias in their medicines, thinking they could "clean" the body out. White settlers soon followed their example. People of those days felt that vomiting and violent bowel movement got rid of harmful substances in the body. Indian tobacco is still listed in the U.S. Pharmacopoeia, the list of officially-approved drugs.

In pioneer days, lobelia was one of the favorite home remedies. Unfortunately, people were often given too strong a dose, and some died. The moral is: don't try to make home remedies from the lobelias—or anything else—in your garden.

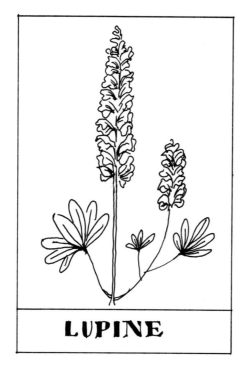

LUPINE

LUPINE. One of the prettiest sights on the rangelands of the West is the wild lupines in bloom, dotting the ground with patches of purple, blue, pink, or white. Sheep love to nibble on the leaves and pea-like seed pods. For thousands of sheep, this is a deadly snack, for some lupines contain a nerve poison. The poison is deadly if a large amount is eaten at one time, and a hungry animal often does just that. The poison affects humans as well as sheep.

Lupines belong to the pea family, and they are a large group. Some species are native to Europe. About 100 are native to the western United States and Canada. Some kinds are not poisonous, and in fact they were once raised in Europe as cattle fodder. Unfortunately, it is very difficult to tell the poisonous and harmless kinds of lupines apart.

Scientists have found, too, that the poisonous kinds are less dangerous at some times of the year. The amount of rainfall and sunshine they get also has an effect on how poisonous they are.

Lupines are also popular garden flowers, coming in a whole rainbow of colors. Like their wild relatives, they grow 3 to 5 feet tall, with flower spikes tightly packed with blossoms. (There are also dwarf varieties.) Some of the garden lupines are poisonous. The most dangerous parts are the pods and seeds.

Some other names for wild lupines are "wild bean," "blue pea," and "Indian bean." The scientific name, *Lupinus,* is Latin for "wolfish." The Romans made great use of lupines. They used them in medicines for sores and skin troubles. Poor people ate the seeds—first soaking them in water for a long time to get rid of the bitter taste. The dried stalks of lupines were burned as fuel. But even in ancient times, it was known that people were sometimes poisoned by lupines; so it is best to enjoy them for their color alone, not tempt fate by eating them.

MOUNTAIN LAUREL

MOUNTAIN LAUREL and DWARF LAUREL are related to the rhododendron. They seem to be more poisonous than rhododendron, or maybe they are just more attractive to animals. At any rate, they rank much higher as killers of farm animals.

Mountain laurel is a bush that may grow as much as 10 feet tall. It has shiny, pointed leaves that stay on the branches all year round. It flowers in early summer. The blossoms are pink to white, with small, spotted markings of a deeper color. Because of the flowers' patterns, it is sometimes called "calico bush." (Calico is a kind of cloth with a spotted pattern. A spotted cat is sometimes called a calico for the same reason.)

Dwarf laurel is often called "sheep laurel," "sheepkill," and "lambkill." It, too, is evergreen, and grows to about 4 feet tall. It likes poor soil and is found in abandoned fields and pastures.

Animals usually stay away from the laurels because their leaves are tough and leathery. But they eat them in winter and early spring when they are the only green thing around.

OLEANDER

OLEANDER is an ornamental shrub that grows in warm climates. It originally grew in the lands around the Mediterranean Sea. Oleanders are now raised widely in the southern United States and in California, where they can grow out-of-doors. They are often used as hedges because their slender, pointed leaves are evergreen and make a good screen the year round. In the North, people grow oleanders as house plants. Oleander flowers are usually pink, white, or yellow, and they are the main reason why the plant is raised.

Unfortunately, oleanders are among the most poisonous of plants. All parts of them are dangerous, even when they are dead and dried up. They contain natural chemicals known as *cardiac glycosides*. These chemicals are powerful poisons. They cause severe vomiting and diarrhea. They also slow and weaken the beating of the heart. In a bad case of oleander poisoning, the victim may die of a stopped heart.

Oleanders are so poisonous that a single leaf may kill a grown person. People have even been killed when they used oleander twigs for skewers for cookouts. This used to happen especially to soldiers in old-time armies when they cooked meat over their campfires. But in Florida about 25 years ago, a number of persons were poisoned when they roasted hot dogs on oleander sticks.

POTATO

POTATO is one of the most important food plants in the world. Native to the bleak, chilly highlands of the Andes Mountains in South America, it is now grown from the Arctic Circle to the tropics. The potato belongs to the nightshade family, and most parts of the plant contain poisonous chemicals called alkaloids. The vines and fruits—small, greenish berries that form on the vines —are dangerous to farm animals. People, too, have been poisoned by the berries when they ate them by mistake.

The portion we eat—the tuber—is normally free of poison. But green spots on the skin are highly poisonous. These green spots form when the potato is not completely covered by soil and is exposed to sunlight. They also form when potatoes are exposed to strong light during storage. Potato sprouts are also poisonous. All green spots and sprouts should be cut out of potatoes before they are cooked. They should be thrown away, not fed to pets or livestock.

Some scientists say that cooking greened potatoes in water washes out the poison, but it is best not to take chances. Several people have died from eating greened potatoes, and others have become sick.

An interesting thing about the potato is that the tuber, which looks like a swollen root, is not a root at all. It is a special type of stem that grows underground. The plant uses it to store food in the form of starch. The tubers also have "eyes" on their skin. The eyes are sprouts that are just starting to form. They are actually leaf-buds that will sprout into leafy stems and form new potato plants. In fact, the main way of planting potatoes is to cut up last year's potatoes into pieces, with one eye to each piece, and plant these in the ground.

The Indians of the high Andes were raising 240 types of potatoes at the time the Spanish conquered them. There were big potatoes and potatoes as small as a ping-pong ball, white potatoes, pink potatoes, even purple, black, spotted, and streaked potatoes.

The Indians preserved them in various ways. One way was to leave the potatoes out overnight to freeze. The next day, when they thawed out, the Indian farmers trampled them with their feet to squeeze out the water. They repeated this for five days, until the potatoes were quite dehydrated. In this state, they would keep for years. The Inca name for this preparation was *chuño* (pronounced choon-yo). Other tribes probably had different names for it.

Potatoes have many uses. Not only are they human food; they are fed to livestock. Starch and alcohol are made from them, and from these products a long list of other useful chemicals are made.

The Spaniards brought the potato from South America to Europe. For a long time, it was raised only as a curiosity. Many people were afraid of potatoes and thought they caused disease. But it was not until the mid-1700s that Europeans began seriously to grow potatoes as a food crop. Now, as we know, they are one of our basic foods. Just watch out for the green spots and sprouts.

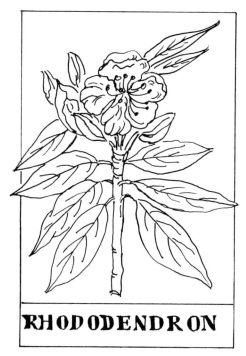

RHODODENDRON

RHODODENDRON is Greek for "rose tree," but rhododendrons are not related to roses at all. They belong to the heath family. Some of their relatives are the azalea, mountain laurel, heather, and blueberry.

Rhododendrons grow wild over large parts of Europe, Asia, and North America. They are also raised for their flowers and evergreen leaves in yards, gardens, and parks. Most of the rhododendrons we see around houses and parks are bushes. But under the right conditions, they grow to the size of a small tree.

Rhododendrons have no tempting fruits to poison unwary people, but the leaves contain a substance that has killed many hungry cows and sheep that browsed on them. The honey of rhododendron flowers is poisonous also. People have been made very sick by eating honey that bees have taken from rhododendron flowers. The poison attacks the nervous system and causes vomiting, diarrhea, and weakness. In severe cases, the victim sinks into a coma and dies.

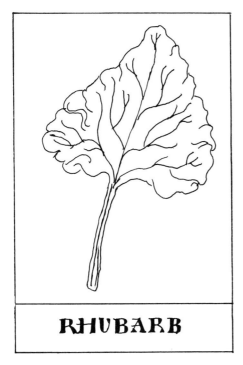

RHUBARB

RHUBARB. A woman was making a rhubarb pie for her family. She chopped up the stalks to cook, and then without thinking, she nibbled at a few of the leaves. She was soon sorry.

Although the stalks of rhubarb are perfectly safe to eat, the leaves contain dangerous amounts of oxalic acid. When swallowed, the oxalic acid passes into the bloodstream. It reacts with the blood to form needle-sharp crystals like those in dumb cane and skunk cabbage. These crystals collect in the kidneys, plugging them up and damaging them. The oxalic acid also affects the blood so that it will not clot properly, causing heavy bleeding.

The symptoms are violent vomiting, diarrhea, nosebleeds, and weakness. Fortunately, people rarely eat rhubarb leaves. If they do, they seldom eat enough to get a deadly dose. But a woman in Montana made a meal of fried rhubarb leaves and died 36 hours later. In England during World War I, a number of people died when an uninformed government official urged them to eat rhubarb leaves to stretch the food supply.

Rhubarb belongs to the buckwheat family and is native to Asia. The Chinese were using rhubarb as a laxative and tonic more than 4,000 years ago. Later, the Greeks and other Europeans learned about it, and rhubarb was a standard remedy until recent times.

At one time rhubarb was raised on a large scale in

China and Russia. This medicinal rhubarb was a different type from our garden rhubarb. It was raised for its roots, which were dug up when they had grown old and large, cleaned and dried, and ground to powder. They were not meant to be eaten. Medicinal rhubarb was so prized by doctors that it was once one of the costliest drugs.

In the United States, rhubarb is eaten as a dessert. It takes a good deal of sugar to overcome the sour taste of rhubarb. But stewed rhubarb, sometimes combined with a fruit, is enjoyed by many people. So is rhubarb pie. In fact, an old name for rhubarb is "pieplant."

SNOW-ON-THE-MOUNTAIN

SNOW-ON-THE-MOUNTAIN. A woman came to her doctor with a puzzling —and very uncomfortable —skin problem. Her skin was covered with a painful, itching, blistery rash. The doctor gave her test after test, but he could not find out what the puzzling ailment was. Then he learned that the woman had a garden that she loved to work in, and that she always had skin inflammation after working in the garden. Skillfully questioning his patient, the doctor found that one of her garden plants was snow-on-the-mountain. It was this plant which caused her rash.

Snow-on-the-mountain belongs to the spurge family, whose milky juice is very irritating to the skin. It grows wild as a weed from Minnesota south to Texas. Easterners thought the two-foot plant with its white-edged green leaves was pretty, and they planted it in gardens as an ornamental. Now plant nurseries sell it all over the country.

People should be very careful in handling snow-on-the-mountain. Its juice not only irritates and blisters the skin, but if it gets into your eyes it can injure them seriously.

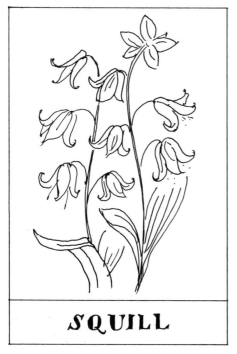

SQUILL

SQUILL is the name of a group of small, spring-flowering plants that belong to the lily family. Many people grow them for a touch of color in early spring. By the middle of summer, their leaves have withered and disappeared. But the following spring, new leaves and flowers sprout again from an underground bulb.

It is this bulb that is the poisonous part of the squill. The bulb contains two poisons: one acts on the heart, and the other causes almost instant vomiting.

The garden squill has a giant cousin known as sea squill, red squill, or sea onion. This plant, which grows around the Mediterranean Sea, has a huge bulb that weighs up to 4 pounds.

Sea squill has been used in medicine for nearly 4,000 years. The ancient Egyptians used it in a remedy for heart trouble (in very small doses because squill is so poisonous). The Greeks thought of it as a kind of miracle drug. But today its main use is in rat poison, under the name of red squill. Rats cannot vomit; so when they eat the poison (mixed with some food they like), they cannot get rid of it. It stays in their bodies until it stops their hearts. However, human beings vomit it up quickly; so very few human deaths have occurred from red squill.

The garden squill plants are not as poisonous as sea squills, but anyone who eats them is still in for an unpleasant experience.

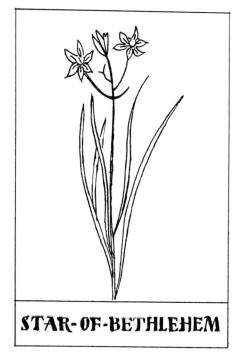

STAR-OF-BETHLEHEM

STAR-OF-BETHLEHEM is named for its white, star-like flowers, which have a stripe of green down the back of each petal. Its scientific name *Ornithogalum*, comes from the Greek words for "bird's milk." This was an old name for the flower.

Native to southeastern Europe and southwestern Asia, Star-of-Bethlehem was brought to the United States as a garden flower long ago. It soon went wild and flourished as a weed in pastures and thickets. It now grows from Newfoundland, Canada in the east to Nebraska and Kansas in the west, and to North Carolina in the south.

Star-of-Bethlehem belongs to the lily family. It grows nearly 1 foot tall, with slender, grass-like leaves. The bulb looks like a small, white onion and contains a poison much like colchicine (*See* Autumn Crocus.) In the United

States, sheep and cattle have been killed by eating Star-of-Bethlehem bulbs that they pulled up accidentally while eating the leaves. In the state of Maryland alone, more than 1,000 sheep were killed by Star-of-Bethlehem in a single year.

The leaves may be poisonous too, though some scientists believe they are harmless. At any rate, the safest thing is to leave them alone.

Star-of-Bethlehem has a first cousin called chincherinchee, which is native to South Africa. Florists sell a great deal of chincherinchee as cut flowers, for the blossoms last for weeks even without water. Chincherinchee is also poisonous, and care should be taken to keep small children and cats away from it.

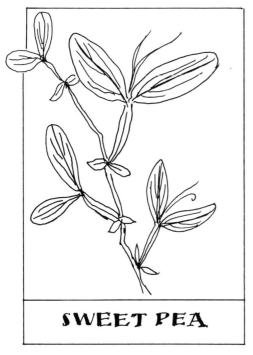

SWEET PEA

SWEET PEA is a relative of our garden peas. It should really be called "sweet-scented pea," because it is named for its fragrance, not its taste.

The sweet pea was originally a wild flower of the island of Sicily. No one paid any attention to it until 1697, when an Italian priest wrote about it in a book on gardens. A few years later, the priest sent seeds to a friend in England. In time, sweet peas became very popular garden flowers. And they still are.

The sweet pea bears pods just like those of garden

peas, and the peas inside look just like the kind we eat. Unfortunately, the sweet pea, like so many other members of the pea family, is not safe to eat. In small quantities its peas are not harmful, but eating big helpings for several weeks has caused paralysis in human beings and animals.

WISTERIA

WISTERIA is a climbing, woody vine that belongs to the pea family. Its blossoms, which appear in early summer, are beautiful. They may be blue, white, purple, or pink. The pods, which follow the blossoms, look like giant, fuzzy pea pods, and the seeds look like lima beans. But neither the pods nor the seeds are for eating.

Wisteria contains substances that poison the digestive system, causing severe vomiting and diarrhea. Children have been poisoned by eating wisteria pods or seeds, sometimes badly enough to be put in the hospital.

The plant is native to China, and was brought to the United States by Yankee trading ships in the early 1800s.

Wisteria is named for a Philadelphia doctor, Caspar Wistar, who lived from 1761 to 1818. Wistar was interested in every kind of science, not just in medicine, and he liked to help poor scientists. One of those he helped, an English botanist named Thomas Nuttall, named the beau-

tiful Chinese vine after his friend. Nuttall was a fine botanist but a poor speller. And so it is that the plant is now known as wisteria instead of wistaria.

YEW

YEW is a tree that is grown as an ornamental. It is an evergreen, with plump, rather soft needles with blunt points. The needles are very dark green on the top side and lighter colored on the underside. Unlike most needle-leaved trees, the yew does not bear cones. Its seeds come wrapped in juicy, red berries almost as big as marbles.

Birds love these berries and can feast on them without harm. But the seeds are poisonous. Sometimes children are poisoned by eating the red berries and swallowing the seeds. The bark and needles of the yew are poisonous too. They are very dangerous to livestock, because hungry animals are apt to eat the needles and bark.

The poisonous substances in the yew act on the nervous system, slowing the heart and then stopping it. This happens to animals and people alike.

Yews are mostly native to Europe and Asia. But many people in the United States and Canada plant them on their lawns and next to their houses for their beauty. There are also varieties of yew that are bushes instead of trees. Many people use them for hedges.

The hard, strong wood of the yew tree was once used for fine furniture, carriage axles, and bows. In England, the finest bows were always made of yew. Because of their dark color, yews were often planted in churchyards as symbols of mourning.

Plants of Woods, Fields, and Roadsides

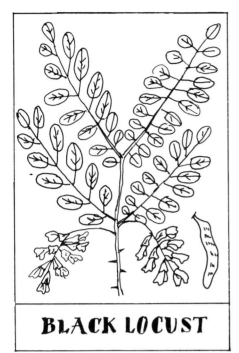

BLACK LOCUST

BLACK LOCUST. On a fall day in 1887, workmen were putting in black locust logs as fence posts at an orphans' home in Brooklyn, New York. (Locust wood is hard and heavy, and lasts for years without rotting. It makes the best fence posts of any trees in the United States). Some of the boys at the home chewed bark the workmen had stripped from the logs. Thirty-two of the boys became ill. Two almost died.

The boys fortunately recovered. But hundreds of horses, mules, cows, and sheep that have eaten the young shoots or the bark of black locust trees have died. For the black locust contains a dangerous poison that causes vomiting, coldness of the hands and feet, and near-unconsciousness. In very severe cases, death is the result. One of the symptoms of locust poisoning is that the pupils of the victim's eyes open very wide. Knowing this may help you to identify a case of locust poisoning.

The black locust belongs to the pea family. Locusts have compound leaves made up of many small, oval-shaped leafllets on a long stem. The young branches and trunks carry hard, sharp thorns that disappear when the trees grow older. In early summer, black locust has big clusters of white, fragrant blossoms. Later, it bears its seeds in long, flat, dark pods. The seeds look something like black lima beans. Don't eat them. They are as poisonous as the bark.

The black locust originally grew in the Appalachian Mountains, from Pennsylvania to Alabama. It also grew in the area where Missouri, Arkansas, and Oklahoma come together. But people outside those areas planted locust trees in their yards, and so they spread far beyond their original range. Locusts send out underground runners, and new trees sprout from these; so one locust tree can give birth to a whole grove.

Today, you may find black locust trees in most states of the United States. They grow in woods, in abandoned fields, along roadsides, and on old homesteads.

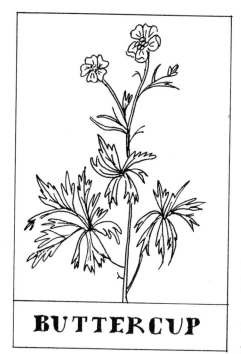

BUTTERCUP

BUTTERCUP. What could look more innocent than a buttercup, with its shinny, golden-yellow petals? Almost everyone who has lived or visited in the country has played the old game of holding a buttercup flower under another person's chin. If the flower casts a yellow glow on the other person's chin, the story goes, they like butter.

But the rest of the buttercup plant is not to be played with. The juice of its leaves and stems contains a poisonous, oily substance that is very irritating. Cows and other animals that accidentally eat buttercups get severe irritations of their mouths, throats, and digestive systems. The poison probably acts the same way in human beings. Some kinds of buttercups have a juice so irritating that it can burn and blister the skin.

About 40 different kinds of buttercups grow wild in the United States and Canada. They range in height from 1½ to 6 feet. Their flowers have 5 petals, and most are yellow. A few have white flowers. Buttercups like lots of moisture; so they grow in marshy meadows, along the banks of streams, and other damp spots. The scientific name of the buttercup, *Ranunculus,* is Latin for "little frog." The name probably comes from the fact that buttercups and frogs like the same kinds of places to live in.

In Europe a few hundred years ago, buttercups were considered one of the most poisonous plants there was. Nevertheless, they had their uses.

People suffering from a toothache often crushed buttercup plants with salt and tied the mess around one of their fingers. Soon the burning juice caused such pain in the finger they forgot the pain in the tooth!

Beggars would sometimes make poultices of crushed buttercup and place them on their skins to make ugly-looking sores. This made people pity them and give them money.

CHOKECHERRY

CHOKECHERRY. Many a person who has spit out one of the mouth-puckering fruits of the chokecherry tree in disgust must have wondered whether it was poisonous. Actually the flesh of chokecherries is not poisonous, bad as it tastes. But the seeds of the fruit and the leaves of the trees contain a deadly chemical called hydrogen cyanide.

A victim of cyanide poisoning becomes nervous, staggers, suffers convulsions, and has difficulty breathing. Death usually occurs within an hour.

The chokecherry tree is small and scraggly. Sometimes it only grows to the size of a bush. The bark is gray, which helps to tell it apart from the many other kinds of wild cherry trees that grow in North America.

The cherries are about the size of a small pea, and they turn nearly black when they are ripe. With enough sugar ripe chokecherries can be made into a tasty jelly. Hikers and country children sometimes eat them raw. Unfortunately, some people swallow the seeds along with the flesh and become victims of cyanide poisoning. A number of children who ate too many chokecherries without spitting out the seeds have died. However, swallowing one or two chokecherry pits won't harm you.

One final warning: there are nearly 50 species of wild cherries growing in North America—cousins of the chokecherry. All of them can be dangerous if you eat the wrong parts.

DEADLY NIGHTSHADE

DEADLY NIGHTSHADE is one plant that lives up to its name. The nightshades have been known to be dangerous for many centuries. The name "nightshade" itself comes from Old English, and is probably a way of describing the plant's poisonous nature.

Deadly nightshade is native to America. It grows mainly in woods and meadowlands. A very close relative from Europe has also gone wild here and grows mainly in land that has been torn up for farming or building. The plants grow from 6 inches to 2 or 3 feet tall and have white flowers. The berries, green when first formed, turn a shiny black or dark purple when ripe. They measure about ¼ inch to ¾ inch in size.

All parts of the plant are poisonous, and animals have been poisoned by eating the leaves. But the berries are the most dangerous part for human beings, since they are the only part of the plant that humans would normally eat. The poison, a narcotic, is very similar to that of jimson weed, and the effects are the same.

A close relative of deadly nightshade is a European plant called *belladonna*. *Belladona* is Italian for "beautiful lady," and it got its name because women used to put drops of belladonna extract in their eyes to make their pupils big and wide. This was considered beautiful a few centuries ago. The eye-widening action of belladonna comes from a substance called *atropine*. Belladonna extract is made from the roots and leaves of the plant. Eye doctors use it today when they examine your eyes. By opening up the pupil, the atropine makes it possible for the doctor to examine the inside of the eye. Otherwise, the pupil would close up when the doctor shined his light into the eye, and he could see nothing.

Belladonna is also used in very small dosages to treat stomach cramps, as it quiets the nerves.

Deadly nightshade was used by various Indian tribes. Some boiled the roots for a medicine to treat worms in children. The fresh leaves, crushed and mixed with grease, made a pain-killing ointment, due to the narcotic action of the poison.

The Rappahannock Indians of Virginia made a weak tea from deadly nightshade leaves to cure sleeplessness. But too much of this "cure" can put a person to sleep forever.

Nightshades belong to the same big plant family as the tomato, tobacco plant, jimson weed, potato, and eggplant, to name just a few members. There is a non-poisonous strain of nightshade that is sometimes raised in gardens. Some people use it to make pies and jam. Most people, however, do not trust it.

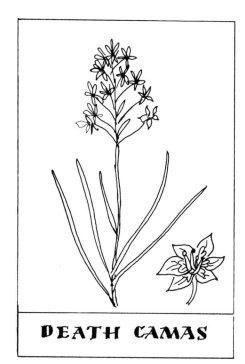

DEATH CAMAS

DEATH CAMAS is a wild relative of the hyacinth. It grows 1 to 2 feet tall, with long, slender leaves and white flowers. Underground it has a bulb like an onion. This bulb contains several nerve poisons, which cause vomiting, muscular weakness, and weakening of the heart. The victims often have trouble breathing. If they are badly poisoned, they become unconscious and may die.

Death camas is most common in the West, but some species of it grow in the East. Its name comes from a Nez Percé Indian word, *quamash*. This was the Indian's name for a related plant whose roots were good to eat. In fact, the Indians of the Rocky Mountains lived on camas roots for much of the year. The non-poisonous camas has blue flowers, not white ones; so the plants are easy to tell apart when they are blooming. Unfortunately, they are not easy to tell apart at other times of the year. Sometimes the Indians ate the wrong one. White settlers in the West often were poisoned by death camas, too.

Occasional cases of death-camas poisoning still occur. Usually the victims are children, who eat the bulb thinking it is an onion. Cattle, horses, and sheep are also poisoned by eating death camas as they graze on the range.

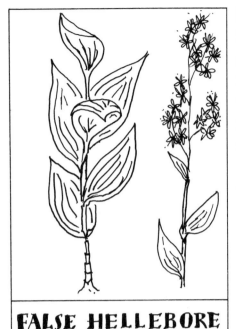

FALSE HELLEBORE

FALSE HELLEBORE belongs to the lily family. It grows in low, wet places from Quebec, Canada, west to Minnesota and south as far as Maryland. In the mountains, where it is cool, it grows as far south as Georgia.

False hellebore grows from 3 to 7 feet tall, with big, handsome green leaves. However, its small, greenish flowers, would never take a prize in a flower show. Both the leaves and flowers turn dark as they age. This probably gave the plant its scientific name, *Veratrum viride*, which is Latin for "Truly black green one."

The Algonquin Indians called the plant *poke,* and one of its names today is "Indian poke." Indians of many tribes used false hellebore as medicine. Most of all, they used it as an emetic and a powerful laxative. (An emetic is a drug that makes you vomit). They also used a powder of the dried leaves mixed with raccoon or wildcat grease to dust on wounds. For aches and pains, they scratched the sufferer's skin over the aching part and rubbed in the powder-grease mixture. They used the powdered roots to take away the pain of a toothache.

They also boiled the roots and used the extract to kill lice on children's heads, to kill caterpillars that attacked their gardens, and to treat corn seeds before planting. The root was ground to powder, mixed in with the seed corn and planted with it. When birds came to eat the newly planted seeds, the hellebore acted like a narcotic.

The birds became so dizzy they could not fly. When they recovered, they very seldom came back for more.

White settlers learned the uses of false hellebore from the Indians, and used it a great deal in medicine themselves. Unfortunately, country folk sometimes gave the patients overdoses of the medicine, and they became very sick or even died. However, false hellebore extract, highly purified, is still used in medicine to treat high blood pressure and heart conditions.

All parts of the false hellebore are poisonous, especially the roots. You should never try it in a salad of wild greens. A human being has to eat a great deal of false hellebore to die, but it doesn't take much to make you awfully sick.

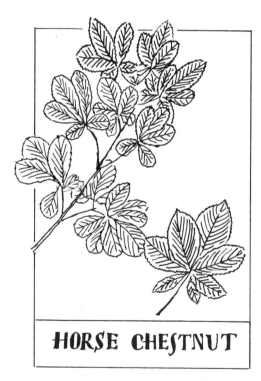

HORSE CHESTNUT

HORSE CHESTNUT and BUCKEYE. The horsechestnut tree is named for its shiny, brown nuts, which look like chestnuts and come in spiny burrs like those of chestnuts. The "horse" part of the name may come from an old belief that the leaves could be fed to horses.

The horse chestnut is native to Europe, but in the United States it is planted along streets and roads because of its flowers. No one who has ever seen a horse chestnut in bloom, covered with big, candlelike spikes of pink or white blossoms, will forget the sight.

There are also 25 native North American species of

horse chestnut. These are known as BUCKEYES because the nuts have a large, pale scar which early settlers thought looked like a deer's eye. Most buckeyes have yellow flowers. Early settlers in Ohio found so many buckeyes growing there that they nicknamed Ohio the "Buckeye State."

The nuts, bark, and young leaves of horse chestnut and buckeye contain a poison that causes vomiting, twitching, and paralysis. Farm animals and children have been poisoned by them. A west-coast species, the California buckeye, yields poisonous honey.

The Indians had a way of treating buckeye nuts to remove the poison. First they roasted the horse chestnut nuts, then mashed them, and finally poured water through the pulp for several days. This was a very laborious way to make food, but the nuts were not safe to eat without this treatment.

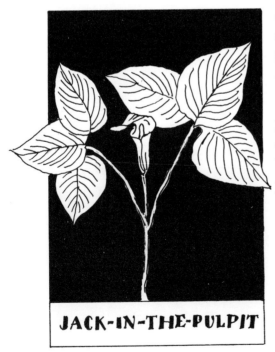

JACK-IN-THE-PULPIT

JACK-IN-THE-PULPIT and its bad-smelling relative SKUNK CABBAGE grow wild over the eastern half of the United States. They prefer low, swampy ground or rich, moist woodlands. But they will grow even higher on hillsides if they get enough moisture in spring and shade in summer.

Both these plants belong to the arum family. They contain the same needle-sharp crystals of calcium oxalate that make their relative dumb cane so dangerous. (*See* Dumb cane).

Jack-in-the-pulpit is named for the fat, yellow spike that stands upright inside the plant's hood. This spike reminded early settlers of a preacher standing in his pulpit. Actually, it is the male part of the plant's flower. The female flowers are down inside the hood, around the base of the spike, so that you have to peer inside to find them. The hood itself is colorfully striped with bands of green and purple. Its purpose is probably to protect the flowers from freezing temperatures, for Jack-in-the-pulpit appears in early spring, before the danger of frost is past in the colder parts of the country.

The hood sits on top of a fleshy stem that grows one to three feet tall. Later in the season, the Jack-in-the-pulpit puts out three large, green leaves. In fall, the hood dries up, and you can see a tightly packed bunch of bright red berries, the Jack's fruit. You may be tempted to try these inviting-looking berries. It's a mistake. They are fiery-hot and irritating to the mouth and throat.

American Indians sometimes ate the bulbous root of the Jack-in-the-pulpit. In fact, another name for Jack-in-the-pulpit is Indian Turnip. But they were careful to cook it first to destroy the poison. Baking the root for at least 24 hours or drying it out makes it safe to eat. But boiling does nothing for it. One expert on wild foods tried boiled Jack-in-the-pulpit roots, and found that they still set his mouth and throat on fire. He could not eat them until they had been dried out for several months in his attic.

Some Indian tribes used Jack-in-the-pulpit as medicine. For instance, the Omahas treated headaches by sprinkling powdered Jack-in-the-pulpit root on the patient's forehead. This caused his skin to sting and burn so painfully that he forgot the pain inside his head! The Omahas called this remedy "coyote medicine," perhaps because it had such a nasty bite.

White people also used Jack-in-the-pulpit in medicines. One use was in remedies to make a sick person sweat and "break" a fever. It was also used to make patients cough up phlegm. A third use was as a heating salve to relieve aches and pains. (Heating salves are still advertised on TV today. Watch the smiles on the faces of the actors in the commercials as they show the audience how the salve gives "prompt relief.")

SKUNK CABBAGE is one of the very first plants to appear in the spring. Its hoods often push up while there is still snow on the ground. The hoods are pretty to look at, with their deep, rich striped and mottled colors. Red, purple, brown, green, and yellow may all be on one skunk-cabbage hood. But if you step on one, you'll quickly see why this plant is called skunk cabbage! It does smell just like a skunk, though not as strong.

Skunk cabbage smells so unpleasant that no one would eat it except on a dare. People who tried it have reported that a single mouthful made their mouths and throats raw and burn for hours.

As the weather warms up, the skunk-cabbage root sends up a slender, green cone of rolled-up leaves. As the plant grows, the cone swells up like a young cabbage head. In summer, it unfolds into large, floppy leaves, which die and wither away in fall. But at any time of the year, no real cabbage ever smelled like skunk cabbage.

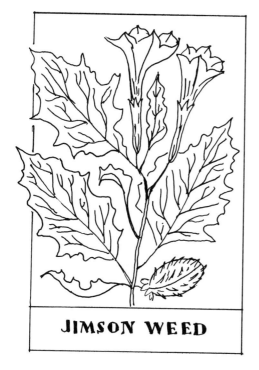

JIMSON WEED

JIMSON WEED is a member of the nightshade family. Some scientists believe it originally came from Asia. But the first English settlers at Jamestown, Virginia, in the early 1600s, found it growing wild there. Some settlers, not knowing the plant was poisonous, stewed up a mess of the big leaves, thinking it was some kind of wild spinach. For the next few days, the narcotic effects of the plant made them temporarily insane.

A historian wrote not long afterward: " . . . they turn'd natural Fools upon it for several days. One would blow a Feather in the Air; another would dart Straws at it with much Fury; and another stark naked was sitting in a Corner, like a Monkey grinning and making Mows (faces) at them . . . In this frantik Condition they were confined, lest they in their Folly should destroy themselves."

Thanks to this incident and others like it, the troublesome plant became known as the Jamestown weed. In time, "Jamestown" was shortened to "Jimson." Other names of this plant include apple of Peru, angel's trumpet (for the trumpet-shaped flowers), stinkweed, and thorn apple. The last name comes from the Jimson weed's fruit, which is spiny, green, and egg-shaped, about the size of a walnut.

Jimson weed grows best in rich soils, but it will also grow in almost any open space where it is not disturbed.

The plant grows 4 to 5 feet tall, with large, coarse leaves and sweet-smelling, trumpet-shaped flowers about 4 inches long. The flowers are usually white but may be purple.

Jimson weed contains several poisonous alkaloids, and every part of the plant is poisonous. The first thing victims notice is that they feel terribly thirsty. Even drinking huge quantities of water will not relieve their thirst. Then the pupils of their eyes dilate (open wide), and they have trouble seeing. If they live, as many do, their pupils may stay dilated for as long as two weeks. Their skin becomes flushed. As the poison works on their nervous systems, they begin to have hallucinations—that is, they "see" and "hear" imaginary things. They may run a temperature, and their heartbeat may become rapid and weak. If they have taken too large a dose, they go into convulsions, then coma and death.

Usually it is children who are poisoned by eating the fruits, seeds, or leaves of the plant, or by sucking the sweet nectar from the flowers. But one grown man in Tennessee nearly killed himself and his entire family in a freakish experiment. He grafted a tomato vine onto the stem of a Jimson weed (the two plants are related), hoping to get bigger tomatoes and somehow make them more frost-proof. The poisonous substance from the Jimson weed passed into the tomatoes, and a single tomato sent two members of the family to the hospital and made the other three very sick.

Jimson weed's scientific name is *Datura stramonium*. Closely related plants grow in Asia and South America. All contain the same poisons. Jimson weed and its relatives have also been used in medicine. The Aztec Indians of Mexico, for example, used it in pain-relieving ointments. Many Indian tribes smoked the dried leaves to treat asthma, and the plant is still used for this purpose. Country folk used to mash the leaves to make a poultice to put on annoying insect bites. And important medical drugs are still made from Jimson weed.

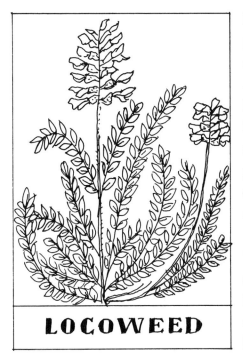

LOCOWEED

LOCOWEED. No book on poisonous plants would be complete without locoweed. Although no human beings have ever been poisoned by locoweed (it's not the sort of plant even a starving person would eat), it is one of the biggest killers of cattle, horses, and sheep.

Loco is Spanish for "crazy," and animals poisoned by locoweed certainly behave as if they had gone mad. They stare blankly as if they do not see. Then suddenly they become frightened at some slight noise or movement and become wild and uncontrollable. At first, they may try to leap over pebbles on the ground and run through fences, because their vision is affected. Later, they lose control of their muscles and tremble and stagger helplessly. In the last stages of poisoning, they stop eating and drinking, and of course die. Fortunately, animals can be saved if they are taken away in time from pastures where locoweeds grow.

There are many kinds of locoweeds. All of them belong to the pea family. Most of them belong to the genus *Astragalus,* whose name comes from the Greek word for an animal's knucklebone. Some belong to the genus *Oxytropis,* which is Greek for "sharp point."

Locoweeds poison the nervous system. They do this

in one of two ways. Some kinds of locoweeds contain a narcotic chemical which causes the "blind staggers" and other symptoms of loco poisoning. Others absorb from the soil a rare element called *selenium*. Selenium is very useful to man. Is is used in photoelectric cells, in solar power cells, and to take the green out of glass or to color it red. But it is extremely poisonous. In fact, because selenium is so poisonous, it is used in special paints for ships' bottoms to prevent seaweed and barnacles from growing on them.

Locoweeds grow in dry areas of the West. They usually grow from 6 to 18 inches high, and their flowers may be purple, white, or yellow, depending on the kind of plant. Animals will not eat them if they can find better food, but once they have begun to eat locoweed, they become addicted to it. In this way, they hasten their own suffering and death.

MAY-APPLE

MAY-APPLE grows in moist, rich woods over the eastern part of North America, from Quebec, Canada, to Florida and west to Minnesota and Texas.

Early in spring, the roots of the may apple send up one or two big, umbrella-like leaves. Plants with one leaf do not have any flowers, but the ones with two leaves bear a single white blossom at the fork of the leaf stems. The blossom smells very sweet. If it is fertilized, it develops into a berry the size and shape of an egg. When this berry ripens in the fall, it turns lemon-yellow. The plants grow from 12 to 20 inches tall.

The fruits can be eaten when they are ripe, but they are poisonous when green. The rest of the plant—leaves, stems, and especially roots—contains a resinous substance that causes diarrhea and vomiting. Indians and country folk used to eat the fruits, and wild-food fans do so today. Sometimes people make may-apple marmalade from the fruit.

The Indians used may-apple root as a laxative. White settlers followed their example, and doctors also used may apple in medicine. May-apple extract is still listed as an official drug in the U.S. Pharmacopoeia. And modern scientists are experimenting with a new use for may- apple, in treating some kinds of cancer.

MUSHROOMS

MUSHROOM. Mushrooms are tasty, nutritious, and non-fattening. The trouble is that it is very difficult to tell the poisonous kinds from the non-poisonous kinds. Some of the poisonous mushrooms look exactly like some safe-to-eat ones, and even experts are sometimes fooled. As a result, many people are poisoned each year by eating wild mushrooms.

Because it is so tricky to identify mushrooms, the safest thing is to leave all wild mushrooms alone. Most kinds of poisonous mushrooms are not deadly, but there are plenty that will make you violently sick.

Mushrooms are interesting plants. They are fungi, which means that they have no chlorophyll (the substance that makes plants green) and they cannot make their own food as green plants do. Instead, they feed on decaying plant and animal remains in the soil.

The mushroom we see growing above ground is actually only a small part of the mushroom plant. Most of the plant is a mass of slender, root-like threads that spread far out beneath the surface of the ground to gather moisture and nourishment. At certain times of the year, when the mushroom plant is ready to reproduce, the threads send up small, button-like growths which quickly swell up to full mushroom size.

As the mushrooms ripen, they produce tiny, dust-like spores from which new mushroom plants will grow. They release the spores in a cloud of fine dust that the wind carries away to new growing places. An average-sized mushroom may produce as many as 2 *billion* spores. Most of the spores die because they do not fall on the spot where growing conditions are exactly right. Otherwise the world would have a lot more mushrooms than it does. If you step on a ripe puffball (a fungus related to mushrooms), you will see a cloud of spores puff out.

There are many old-time "rules" for telling safe mushrooms from poisonous ones. Do not trust these "rules." They don't work. Stick to the mushrooms you get at the store.

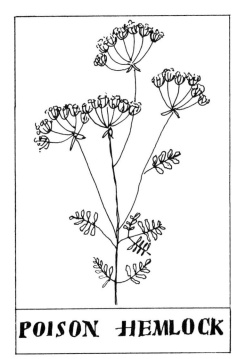

POISON HEMLOCK

POISON HEMLOCK, WATER HEMLOCK, and FOOL'S PARSLEY are three related poisonous plants that grow as weeds. In spite of the name *hemlock,* they have nothing to do with the hemlock tree. Instead, they belong to the same family as carrots and parsley. The scientific name for this family is *Umbelliferae,* which is Latin for "umbrella-bearers." The name comes from the shape of their flower-heads, which look a little bit like an opened umbrella or sunshade.

Poison hemlock grows along roadsides and ditches, the edges of fields, and similar places. It has lacy, fern-like leaves. Its main stem is thick and tall—from 4 to 10 feet—and almost always covered with purple spots. Both stems and leaves are smooth, which is a clue to telling poison hemlock apart from some related plants that look like it. Identifying the plant correctly may save someone's life, for the treatment is different for different poisons.

The tall main stem bears clusters of small, white flowers. A rosette, or circle, of leaves about 3 feet tall grows around the base of the main stem. All the stems of poison hemlock are hollow. Children have been poisoned by using them for blowguns or whistles.

The root looks like a white carrot; sometimes it is forked. It has a disgusting smell that prevents most people from eating it. In fact, the whole plant has the same sickening "mousy" odor. Yet people are sometimes poisoned when they mistake the leaves for wild parsley, the roots for parsnips, or the seeds for anise seed (used to flavor food).

The seeds and leaves are the most poisonous parts of the poison hemlock plant. They contain at least 5 different poisons. All of them act on the nervous system. Hemlock poisoning proceeds by stages. First the victims become nervous. Then they tremble. The next stage is loss of control of the muscles, especially of the legs. The pupils of the eyes widen. Then the heartbeat weakens and slows. The victims become cold, then unconscious. Finally they die when the breathing muscles stop working.

Not everyone who chews on a leaf of poison hemlock dies. But it does not take much to make a fatal dose.

Poison hemlock is native to Europe. It has been known as a poison for thousands of years. The ancient Greeks brewed a deadly drink from it which they used to execute criminals and other "troublemakers," such as people who did not agree with them. The famous Greek philosopher Socrates was forced to drink hemlock poison when he critized the government of his city, Athens. People also used hemlock to get rid of anyone they didn't like.

Long ago, poison hemlock was brought to the United States, probably to be used in medicine. In small, carefully administered doses, the poison acts as a sedative. The plants soon went wild and spread until poison hemlock now grows over most of the United States and southern Canada. Some people, believe it or not, grow it in their gardens because of its decorative leaves.

Water hemlock looks very much like poison hemlock and grows to about the same size. As its name hints, it grows only in ground that is wet at least part of the year. You will find it along streams, in swampy fields, and similar places. It is native to North America as well as to Europe.

Water hemlock has a few features that help identify it. One is that its main stem is thick at the bottom. Another is that it has a bunch of small, fleshy roots, usually 2 to 3 inches long. If the roots or lower stem are cut open, droplets of a yellow, oily fluid ooze out. This yellow fluid contains the poison, which causes violent and painful convulsions. The victims may want to vomit but cannot, because their mouths are clamped shut. Death may come as swiftly as 15 minutes after poisoning, or it may take as long as 8 hours.

Many people have been killed by eating the roots of water hemlock, which are said to taste sweet and pleasant. But one root is powerful enough to kill a cow. In fact, one of water hemlock's nicknames is "spotted cowbane." Another is "beaver poison."

Fool's parsley looks rather like an overgrown parsley plant about one or two feet tall. Like poison hemlock, it has a disgusting smell. Yet people have been poisoned when they mistook its leaves for parsley or its roots for radishes.

Experts disagree on how poisonous fool's parsley is. Some say that it can be fatal. Others say that it causes temporary paralysis but that the victim recovers.

Fool's parsley is native to Europe but was brought to the United States long ago. Its seeds probably came by accident in hay that was used to pack china and other breakable things when they were sent by ship. Now it grows wild in northeastern United States and southeastern Canada. Sometimes it turns up in gardens as a weed.

POISON IVY

POISON IVY, POISON OAK, and POISON SUMAC. No one has ever died from the effects of poison ivy, but no other plant has caused so much discomfort and annoyance to so many people. Every year, about two million Americans come down with a case of ivy poisoning.

The symptoms are all too familiar: a blistery rash and itching that is often unbearable. Many victims swell up in the affected area. Some run a fever, and a few are so severely affected that they must be taken to a hospital.

The cause of this discomfort is an oily substance in the sap of the plant, which causes an allergic reaction when it touches the skin of a sensitive person. Who is sensitive to the poison (easily affected by it)? About seven out of every ten people; the other three should still be careful around poison ivy, for they can lose their immunity at any time. ("Immune" means that people are not affected by the poison.)

The poison is present in all parts of the plant: leaves, stems, roots, flowers, and fruits. People are usually poisoned by brushing up against the leaves. But many have also been poisoned by pulling up the vines in late fall or winter, when the leaves have dropped off.

Poison ivy grows most often as a vine. It climbs on trees, rocks, and whatever else is handy. When there is nothing to climb, it spreads over the ground, some-times forming a carpet of leaves and stems. Occasionally it grows in the form of a bush.

In any case, the easiest way to recognize poison ivy is by its leaves, which always grow in groups of three, no more and no less. The leaves may be of different shapes: broad, slender, smooth-edged, and jagged-edged. Sometimes leaves of different shapes may grow on the same plant.

Poison ivy lives for many years. As it grows older, its stems become thick and hairy. The hairy stems are another sign that you will recognize. Poison-ivy flowers are small and greenish-white. They are followed by grayish-white berries about the size of a matchhead. Birds are fond of these berries and eat them without harm. In fact, birds are the chief spreaders of poison ivy. The seeds pass through their bodies along with the birds' droppings.

Insects also feed on poison ivy, and some lay their eggs in the tissues of the leaves, causing lumps to form. Cows, goats, and horses browse on poison ivy with no ill effects. Dogs and cats roll in it in safety. Scientists say that their fur protects them by keeping the poisonous oil off their skins. In fact, only man, apes, and monkeys seem to be affected by poison ivy.

This unpleasant plant grows in every mainland state except California and Nevada. It also grows in southern Canada, Mexico, Japan, Taiwan, and parts of mainland China. It grows under almost every sort of condition, from swampland to dry, rocky hillsides. It even grows on beaches at the edge of salt water, which would kill most plants.

Poison ivy belongs to the cashew family. Some of its relatives, besides the tasty cashew nut, are the pista-chio, the mango, and the Japanese lacquer tree, from whose sap the famous black, shiny lacquer is made. All these plants are useful to man. But two more members of the family that are not useful are poison oak and poison sumac, both closely related to poison ivy. Both contain the same kind of oily poison as their relative.

Poison oak is named for the shape of its leaves, which look a bit like oak leaves. However, it is not related to the oaks at all. It usually grows as a bush or shrub. Sometimes, however, it climbs like poison ivy. Again like poison ivy, its leaves grow in threes. They are dark green on top and light underneath and are thick and leathery. Poison oak grows in Washington, Oregon, and California, and in the eastern part of the United States.

Poison sumac grows mostly east of the Mississippi. It likes wet places, such as swamps and stream banks. It almost never grows on land that is high and dry all year round. Poison sumac contains more poison in its sap than poison ivy and poison oak; so it is more dangerous to touch. Fortunately, however, it is not as common as either of its relatives.

Poison sumac grows from 8 to 20 feet tall. It has smooth-edged leaves, with 7 to 13 on each leaf stalk.

There are several kinds of sumac, but only one kind is poisonous. The easiest way to tell them apart when you are standing at a safe distance is by the berries they bear in summer and fall. Poison sumac has loose clusters of cream-colored berries that hang down. The harmless sumacs have tightly-packed clusters of red berries that stand upright.

POKEWEED

POKEWEED. A common weed of the eastern half of the United States and south-eastern Canada, pokeweed is also know as scoke, garget, pokeberry, pigeonberry, and inkberry.

It is native to North America but has relatives in Asia. American pokeweed is cultivated in southern Europe as a food and drug plant, and in England some people grow it as an ornamental.

Pokeweed is hard to miss. The plants may grow as much as 9 feet tall, with bright purple-red stems as thick as a broom handle. Pokeweed is a perennial. Each fall it dies down to the ground, but the root lives through the winter and sends up new stems the next spring. In old plants, the carrot-shaped root grows very large and becomes tough and woody. Pokeweed likes rich soil. It grows in ground that has been recently cleared, in open places in woods, and in fields and barnyards.

Over the summer, pokeweed's small whitish flowers develop into hanging clusters of shiny, purple-black berries with red juice. Birds love the berries, which sometimes make them drunk because of the poison they contain.

Pokeweed contains two poisons. The most poisonous part of the plant is the root, although the seeds are also very poisonous. Pokeweed poison is slow-acting but powerful. A person who eats pokeweed immediately feels a burning sensation in the mouth, but nothing more happens for about two hours. Then the victim begins to suffer painful stomach cramps, vomit violently, and have uncontrollable bowel movements. Sometimes the vision is affected temporarily. Usually people recover in about 24 hours, but some victims have died. Pigs have also died from digging up and eating the roots.

Country people used to eat the young shoots of pokeweed in spring, and some wild-food lovers still do. The shoots (new growths) are said to be safe if they are boiled thoroughly and the water thrown away. People have been poisoned, however, when they mistakenly cooked a bit of the root along with the shoots. Old pokeweed is never safe to eat.

The Indians also used pokeweed shoots as food, and they made dozens of medicines from the plant. They used it to treat rheumatism, skin diseases, and swellings.

Pokeweed's scientific name is *Phytolacca*, which was put together from *phyton*, the Greek word for "plant" and *lacca*, a Latin name for a kind of crimson dye. (The juice of the berries was once used as a dye.) The comon name, *pokeweed*, comes from an American Indian word, *pocan*, which some tribes in Virginia used for any plant that yielded a red dye.

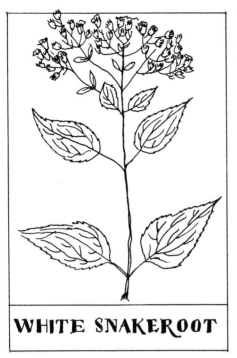

WHITE SNAKEROOT

WHITE SNAKEROOT. As settlers in the early days of the United States cleared farms out of the forest, they sometimes found that their cows got mysteriously sick. The cattle became weak, trembled, and often collapsed and died. The settlers who drank milk and ate butter and cheese from the sick cows also became ill in the same way. They called it the "milk sick," but they did not know what caused it. They did learn that cattle became milk sick only in certain places. Sometimes the settlers moved to escape whatever it was that caused the dreaded milk sick. But most of them did not want to leave the farms they had worked so hard to build in the wilderness. They stayed and took their chances.

Sometimes it was a bad gamble. In certain settlements, more than half the people died of milk sick. Abraham Lincoln's mother was one of the victims, but there were thousands more who never got into the history books.

Unhealthy air, poison ivy, spider webs, and, later on, bacteria were suggested as the cause of the mysterious killer. But the true cause was not discovered until about 1900. It was the innocent-looking wildflower known as white snakeroot.

Snakeroot belongs to the *Compositae* family of plants, which includes daisies, marigolds, thistles, sunflowers, and lettuce, among others. There are many species of snakeroot, most of them harmless. At least 30 species have white flowers, and the only way to identify the poisonous kind is to examine the flowers with a magnifying glass. Even then, only a trained botanist who knows what to look for can tell.

White snakeroot grows wild in moist, open woodlands. For the first few years after the trees are cut down, it grows so thickly that it crowds out most other plants. That is why the pioneer settlers had such trouble with it. By clearing the woods, they gave the plant a chance to take over, and their cattle had little else to feed on. Fortunately, white snakeroot dies out when the land is mowed for hay or cultivated.

The poisonous substance in white snakeroot was not discovered until 1927. It turned out to be a thick, yellow, oily substance which was given the name of *tremetol*. Tremetol causes harmful changes in body chemistry that affect the nervous system.

The chief symptoms in human beings are weakness and prostration, constipation, severe thirst, vomiting, and trembling. Later in the disease, the victims' breath smells of acetone (the liquid used in airplane cement and nail polish). This is due to the chemical changes the poison has caused in their bodies. It is said that in frontier days doctors learned to diagnose milk sick by the odor of their patients' breath. In the last stages of milk sick, the victim goes into delirium and coma before dying.

Milk sick is uncommon nowadays, but cases still occur on small, carelessly run farms. Most victims do not die, but they seldom recover completely. They remain weakened for years or perhaps for life.

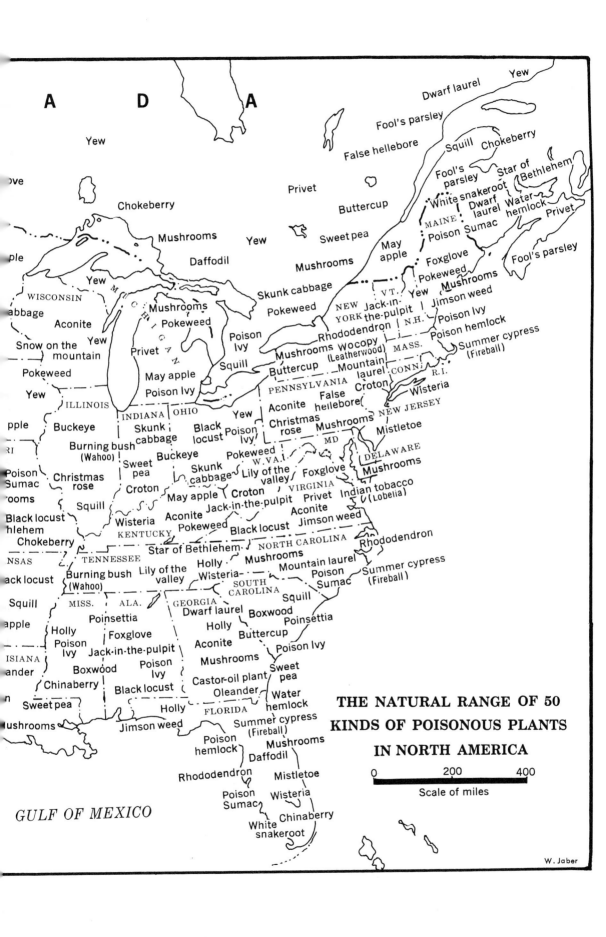

THE NATURAL RANGE OF 50
KINDS OF POISONOUS PLANTS
IN NORTH AMERICA

0   200   400

Scale of miles

W. Jaber

Glossary

ALKALOID——a kind of chemical that occurs naturally in some plants. Many alkaloids are poisonous. Some are narcotics.

ANESTHETIC——a substance that prevents you from feeling pain.

ANNUAL——a plant that lives for only one year.

ASTHMA——a disease in which the patient chokes up and has great trouble breathing.

BUSH——a woody plant with several stems. Bushes may be anywhere from a few inches to 20 feet tall or even more, but they are usually less than 10 feet tall. Even the biggest bushes look different from trees, because trees have only one main stem, which we call the *trunk,* while bushes have more than one. This makes them look "bushy."

CATHARTIC——a powerful laxative. *See* also *laxative.*

COLLAPSE——in medicine, a kind of physical breakdown in which the body cannot perform its functions normally.

COMA——a state of deep unconsciousness. It is impossible to rouse a person from coma.

CONVULSION——when a person has convulsions, his or her muscles clench up violently, relax, and clench up again uncontrollably. This causes the person to thrash about so violently that he or she may injure himself or herself.

DIARRHEA——frequent, very loose bowel movements.

DIGESTIVE——having to do with the digestion of food. A digestive disturbance means that something is wrong with the stomach or intestines.

EMETIC——a substance that causes you to vomit.

EXTRACT——to pull out. In medicine, an extract is a substance that is "pulled out" of plant or animal material by dissolving it and then concentrating it. An extract contains the substance in a purified, strong form.

FOLIAGE——another word for leaves.

HEDGE——a row of bushes or other plants placed close together to serve as a fence.

IMMUNE——not affected by. A person who is immune to measles, for example, will not catch measles even if all of his or her friends come down with them.

INFLAMED——hot, swollen, red, and sore or itchy.

INTENSIVE——very strong or concentrated.

INTESTINAL——having to do with the intestines. The intestines are the tubes that food passes through after it leaves the stomach.

IRRITATING——causing itching or soreness and inflammation.

LAXATIVE——a medicine that causes the bowels to move. A laxative is gentler than a cathartic.

NARCOTIC——a kind of drug that causes numbness and sleepiness. In small doses, narcotics relieve pain and create a feeling of contentment. In large doses, or in long-time use, they are dangerously poisonous.

NERVOUS SYSTEM——all the nerves in the body. It also includes the brain.

OINTMENT——a greasy substance that is put on the skin as medicine or as a cosmetic.

ORNAMENTAL——decorative. An ornamental plant is one that people raise just for its looks—not to eat, not for its shade, not to use any part of it.

PARALYSIS——not being able to move.

PERENNIAL——a plant that lives for more than two years.

PHOTOSENSITIVE——to make sensitive to light. In medicine, the skin of a photosensitized person or animal becomes swollen and inflamed by even a little exposure to sunlight—just like a really severe sunburn.

PLANT——any living thing that cannot move from place to place by its own efforts, has no sense organs, and usually makes its own food by photosynthesis. Trees, bushes, grass, vegetables, and garden flowers are all plants. We usually think of a plant as something that grows in the ground, or sometimes in water.

POULTICE——a wet dressing put over some part of the body to soothe or heal sores, wounds, rashes, and inflammations. Poultices are usually applied hot.

PROSTRATION——an unhealthy state in which the person is so weakened or exhausted that he or she cannot stand up.

PURGATIVE——a substance that causes violent bowel movements; an extremely strong laxative.

PURIFIED——with the impurities taken out; made pure.

RESINOUS——containing a resin. Resins are a kind of naturally occurring chemical made by plants. They are usually sticky when fresh, but after exposure to the air they gradually harden.

SENSITIVE——in medicine, easily affected by or easily harmed by.

SHOOTS——sprouts; new stems or twigs that sprout from the roots, stems, or branches of plants.

SPROUT——a new growth from some part of a plant.

SHRUB——a woody plant, smaller than a tree. It does not climb. A shrub does not necessarily have many branches like a bush, but bush and shrub are often used with similar meanings.

SPECIES——in science, the basic unit of classification for plants and animals. For example, all carrots belong to the same species. All parsnips belong to a different species. All horses belong to one species; all donkeys belong to another species. The next classification above the species is the *genus,* which usually contains two or more closely related species. Next above genus comes *family.* The whole system goes: species, genus, family, order, class, phylum, kingdom.

SYMPTOM——any sign of disease or poisoning. A runny nose, sore throat, and sneezing are *symptoms* of a cold. Symptoms help doctors tell what is wrong with a sick person.

TOXICITY——degree of poisonousness.

TREE——a woody plant with a single main stem, or trunk. To be called a tree, the plant has to be at least 10 or 12 feet tall when it is full-grown.

VINE——a plant with a long, thin, flexible stem that grows along the ground or climbs up trees, rocks, walls, and so on.

WOODY——a woody plant is one whose stems and branches are made of the hard, fibrous substance we call wood.